# At Times End

Gordon Ellis was born in 1948 of Scottish-Irish descent and was brought up between inner city Birmingham and Gourock on the Firth of Clyde, his family having roots in Ballymena in Co.Antrim. He studied philosophy, literature and religion at university and went on to do research in Hindu iconography. He has taught at university in England, practiced as a psychotherapist, and been spiritual director of a Tibetan Buddhist Centre in Cheshire. Poets he has been influenced by include: Ezra Pound, Basil Bunting, W.S.Graham, Ernst Meister, Gunnar Ekelof and Chinese poets of the Tang Dynasty. As well as a number of books of poetry, he has also published several books of essays, including, 'Avoiding Extinction' co-authored with Alexander Matthews. He now lives in South Devon.

# Works by Gordon Ellis

## Prose

Crossing The Ocean of Existence 2003
Cycling Round Existence (Discovering Aspects of the
Psychopathology of Western Civilisation) 2014
Gordian Knots: Essays 2010-2020

## Poetry

Elysian Wiles
The Broken Shards
At Times End
Shades of Non-Existence, Sculptures of the Void

# At Times End

Gordon Ellis

Rootless Tree

www.elysianwiles.com

ISBN: 978-1-9196313-0-1

*'There is also the possibility of mankind's death. Reasons cannot be given why the people now populating the planet and destroying it in every possible way should continue to exist without end.'*

(Letter from Martin Heidegger to Medard Boss, September 8, 1970 from Freiburg)


*'Engel (sagt man) wusten oft nicht, ob sie unter
Lebenden gehn oder Toten.'*

*'Angels, they say, don't know whether it is the living they are
moving among or the dead.'*

(Rainer Maria Rilke,  Duino Elegy 1)

Coherence death.
Own lea. Move-
Meant, move,
m~o~v~e~m~e~n~t
Entowered, entombed
Omphalos. O flowering
Finale, seed of death!
Look - towards sunRise,
Towards sun-
Set, at boundaries and interstices.
Emerging from silence,
From darkness.
Keeping on.
Until timbrel crashes
Under every stone and within.

Ten signs cower, intimidate,
Twoshot.
Twelve labours.
Blood perfumes ground.
Ordeals shedding skin,
After smooth skin.
Body of light revealing,
A body solight.
Twelve days, and the tenth night
Rainbows appear,
Lightning in desolation
Strikes; soundslime and slithering
Another born, borne away, wave after
Wave, unseen again. Command after
Command, all at sea, then engulfed again.

Plague and pestilence
Borne and submissive.
To show - magnanimity.
Those Jakob enslaved
Punished, to free difference.
No-one is the same, not
Even me. No indeed. I am many.

Wordtools, no sand, no glory.
Dynasties destroyed on Whim.
My myth, your history, that
Plagues our common story since.
Only a mouth that talks
On the other side, side of star
Receding, if there was an ever?
Embracing difference,
Both hands, lopped-off.
If not submission then order,
An ordure: lonely flower that falls.

Reasonable these bones:
Make something new
Unrecognisable, whose
Silence only persists. Red-
Hued like Dawn's fingers
Caressing, new life, erecting
Their monument, that only
Mountain sand will tell.
Slipping, Yes slipping through
Those fingers, ribbons of pain.

Necklace of fingers:
These times of disjoint.
Among the bushes
A disembodied smile.
I see where you've been.
Less word than cadaver.
More stone than living flesh.
I caress this absence
Devoid of hope, or fear.
And around us - all around,
The sky's eye closes.

Your expectations suffered
A priapic arousal,
Clearly a world. Disinhibit.
Where one dream solidified.
Where competing dreams had
Jostled, whatever sustained
Them dissolved. An uneasy truce
Excused itself, fawning courtier
Exiting while keeping face.
What might have passed, never arrived.

The arrow is broken, feathers
Become plumage; whatever
Stirred returned to silence.
Water ripples, glistening.
Singing, and only an absence
To respond to, a winnowing shadow.

Only in recollection.
Existing now.
Set like a table's
Repast, trembling:
So much, unconfined
With no keeping - O
See silvery fish darting,
Chiffchaff calling,
Sunshine as day begins.

Searching understones, unique.
In mounds of Earth, disturbed
Soil, buried stars, looking for
Treasures: sheep droppings, cow's
Dung, child's tooth. Remain
Open to rain, ophthalmic disease.
The Night's caress before
Darkness descends with stealth,
Greets you with renewed birth.

A similitude of
Dissimulation.
Random patterns
Execute with grace
Your benedictions.
Fluttering of eyelids
Disturbs the other side
Of the world:
You close up again
Mollusc regina nox.

Not quite stones, or blocks of sound.
Tattered garments strewn
Where imagined landscapes once
Echoed to a dissonance
A mouth sought to form
With insouciance, a sly smile,
And a wound that would not heal.
Engulfing a world already brittle,
Whose bone could not join or confirm.

Neither too great, nor not…
Enough. You expostulate.
Holy words dribble. Stubble
Is all that remains. There
Was a season once, passing
Like a hand over desolation.
Ripples on a forehead, furrows
That refused to yield, and died.

Umbrella, shadows.
In defiance of all.
A mere vacuity:
Cast into a future
As if there were something
Already there, waiting.
Like death in
Every child's first breath.

Mountains haze, this purple dusk
Where everything becomes One.
Or do they ever change?
It's we that change, confuse
Memories embounded by time
With how things are. A trick
Of words' ancestral depositions.
A jackdaw's nest. A negative
That prints inversion. Hollow
Truths that glimmer, then sink.

Certainly, she said,
Beyond doubt.
Or before doubt.
It's hard to know:
I have never felt so sure.
Enclosed within the eye
The world trancefixed.
Unblinking; staring
Into space, beyond dispute.

Voice: *In the desert*
*Nothing grows*. Only artifice.
O my god! I praise…
Your ways. All is welcome:
*Cando… cando*…the last bird calls.
New leaf, still the same.
Until Nothing to turn over;
Soiled, only silence, still.
In the ever-moving sand.

Earth, water, fire, and air,
Gods and humans,
Is something forgotten?
The abacus absolute,
The absolute calculated.
Measures out days and ways.
Eliminates chance for choice.
Time after time, birds:
One chaffinch, two sparrows,
Try flying through clear glass.
Repeated efforts meeting
Renewed failure, once again.

Golden flowers on mandala
Plate of turquoise.
Close your eyes and what is real
Appears: apples, pears,
Grapes, their smell and taste
Pervaded by the scent
Of absence present. In
A gift unimaginable, noble.

A plague upon your House.
The descent from slime
To a higher ground. Dissolved
Into fragmentary particles.
Less viscous, more coarse.
Travelling down a beam of light
You come upon a crossroad.
And in the midst of agitation
Would weep, if you remembered
How. Now, two-dimensional,
With head spiralling through
Spheres of four or more,
All for a point at which to stop.

Velvet esplanades, unworn.
So far to walk.
Behind the moon
Only a vacant stare.
Heavenwards to Temple
Ruin. Your eye would travel
If not blinkered in permanence.
Where grace descends
You ascend: to never meet.

Rose-apple Island.
A beautiful caress.
Seduced by infallible
Laughter, birds call.
Offering pious waffle
Full of intent.
A gotoo sign limits.
And such such red lips,
Rich, deep crimson,
Define the space of
Endless pain, a smile.
Wishing to follow
Some direction, a goal.
Resisting the embrace
Of jungular engulfing.
Yes, you are free.
Go where you like
Be someone other
Than you are. Elsewhere.

No corner on the outside.
Within, a hole with no corner.
Nothing arrested or released,
Nothing doing. O sing to me.
Sing a lullaby to wake-me-up.
From dream to dream.
Stairway to stairway.
I hear a voice, receding:
Vocables turning into clear light.

Never a day passes,
It only seems-to.
I have seen the script
Play out before,
My memory better once.
Tears formed a sculpture,
Crystalline and radiant.
A hesitant reward
For having breathed at last.

The skies are clear.
My eyes
Withdrawn from the world.
Inside, luminous
Offerings: wine and barley,
And gentle sound
Of bees humming.
Nothing flowers
Without celebration.
Each is finite.
Solid, and immobile
In the end, or
Disintegrating. Like
A tissue of lies.

I see waves.
Ululations.
As another hope
Is carried
Out to sea.
Nothing to be
Afraid of now.
Nowhere else
To go. Just void.

Filled with fear.
Creeping poison
Of paralysis.
My worst dreams
Couldn't happen:
They're already here.

*Charlotte*, I know no one
To whom this name attaches
Who is not fictional.
But then, who do I know?
And which story is ever true?

The jagged edge of Night.
Tooth-saw, replete
With half-mothed dream.
Relinquish your febrile hold.
Describe the vacuity
You enter into. Where
Sounds coalesce
Into new forms, complete,
Discrete, and translucent.

A common name, but pointless
Veneer, sculpted of air.
With gossamer streams
Of rainbow tears: drop…drop…drop.
Nothing escapes these hands,
Wrought of fallacious hope,
With which I welcome a new day:
The dawning of vertiginous despair.

The joy of being a carnivore,
Snout up someone's arse.
Should be a flower
Or what I am.
O humble butterfly.
Show me transience
And I will show you a life
On which has shat Aman.

Forgive me your trespasses:
Jackdaws feed on carrion.

As I forgive you mine:
A rabbit's eye, caught frozen.

O yes! Let us forgive everyone,
As we dance, a whirling firebrand.

Blessed are those
Who persecute
The innocent,
For they shall have
Dominion over all
The Earth; and
Blessed the meek,
Who shall be subjugated
And used to fertilise it.
Thy kingdom come:
So the open-hearted
May cry, and their tears
Irrigate the land.
As only the wizened
May excuse this wisdom
In the fires of youth.
And old Jerusalem
Be born again, renewed.
Flesh to flesh,
Dust to dust.
The dumbird sings
A phantasy to
Feast the eyes.
A zoological
Interregnum
That splices tongues.
Terror gives intelligence
Its form. Solace

It's content. The black sun
Leaves us shadowless:
Water turned to oil.

The evocation drifts like juniper smoke
Across abandoned ruins.
You hold mountains in your severed hand,
Smile spreading like sunlight,
Should you chose to masticate.
The distant sound of sheep-bellows,
Sings lullabies to ease you into sleep.
Tomorrow, a new day
Like yesterday. If you dare to hope again
The pain will brand your bones.
And your smile reveal
What you could not conceal, wry
And tightly wrought, like joy cloying.

The sky falls in fragments
Like broken glass, jagged
Edges stained with blood.
Nowhere to walk is safe.
Operetta plays-on nearby,
Downcast, merry, sacro-
Sanct. Exchange glances
Reveals sobriety, newborn
Hope, destined to disshard.
Like insects, figures slide
Disembodied, once endowed
With steepling fingers.
Heavenwards: Nothing
There, just ribboned feet.

It is so quiet, the silence
Is tangible, smooth,
Without edges, translucent.
Nothing is distinguished.
A fish moves, elegantly
Beneath the surface.
I recall nothing that you said.

A buzzard sits, unflinching,
It knows what to do.
It will do no more.
The circumference circumscribes.
I will write my will
Over the Earth's surface,
Beyond the heavens;
And it will fade,
With my last breath, extinguished.

A rash of bluebells in the woods,
And campions in the hedgerows.
And what passes for human-
An outbreak of bucolia.
Recall then, in tranquility,
After the first assumption,
All others refurbished a fantasy.

I discombobulate. No-one is…
The gentian wipes its brow;
The plover world would cry:
The field-ready…city…(disconsolate).

Hibiscus flowers, bittersweet.
Dreams of tattered rags
Relayed in cinemas with empty seats.
Hear the dulcet sound upon the wind,
Amount upon a thermal.
Invisible scent, pervading everywhere.
A first goodbye, and then goodbye again.
Choosing: better not to start.

Words become objects, stones,
Lose their melody, timbre,
Become defences, like walls,
Or weapons to destroy them.
Breathless, like landed fish,
Gutted, decapitated,
Consumed, mere information.
Until a grave informs their rest,
Returning empty to the sand.

1
Chomolungma, the final assault?
Chinese guards
Drab at basecamp.
Peaks enveloped in cloud,
beyond the blue.
It takes your breath away.

3
Entombed, dependent on
The steady rhythmic action
of another's foot.
All life seen through
A narrow plastic window.

4
You have never been
So close to death,
So dependent on another
Since you were born before.
Remember?

7
At Tingri, cut, cut, cut,
Until nothing is left,
offering, and radiance.
A disembodied smile.
O happy days!

10
While in Lhasa, theme-park,
Parade ground, super highway,
Qinghai railway,
Brings *La vie moderne*.
More opportune.
High heels, short skirts adorning
Han chicks, tottering up
Potala steps.

16
Slow spread of disease that
Suffocates and kills.
Especially the old, ancient,
And the wise.

25
Played-out in holographic realism.
The final assault
                    Or one of many.

Who has seen the wind
Or heard the agony of words?
The bird seizes the worm
And shakes. In serried ranks
Prophet after profit fails.
And yet, and yet, I gain the world.
Reveal only flesh you can,
Eyes beckon, the lighthouse
Warms, both blinking danger,
Embracing, embraced, alone.

The dove released from the hawk's grip,
Flies off to rest on an acer branch,
Leaving feathers for another's nest.
Blissful unawareness of their provenance,
So sleep comes quickly. Release
The present moment and the traffic floods,
Water infused with blood, and oblivion.

Within the space of infinite hospitality,
All is welcome, unpolluted, without
Identity, indiscriminately accepted
Without bias, without judgement, loved.
Free of imagination's constraints, like
A mother unconditional with her child
Arises tenderly, wide as the sky, beyond
Mere thinking and evaluation, just-good.
Remaining in the mountains like a wild deer.

You called, I didn't hear until
You called no more. More heard
Than hearing, more hardened than
Sodden memories, regurgitated fear.
O thrice born! Once deceived in
Euphonious polysemy, no curlew.
Now the open space of possibility:
What future flight alights, what tear?

Heavy rain falls, strong wind
Blasts the rowan. A chaffinch
Hunts among stones. No-one
Moves, nothing else is moving.
What are you waiting for?
Nothing to wait for or do.
Just let it all go - like the wind.

House martins cartwheel in the sky
Above the farm. Pheasants call
In fields, safe from harm.
The precious ampersand, no man
Shall sunder: the world tumbles
Onto a blank page, not at random.
Hidden laws will shape the word
You say, but not the thoughts
You might have had. Figures on
Ground dissolve like salt in water.
After the rain, sun, then insect swarms.

The angel of hypocrisy hangs
Over Ballymena. Good people
See nothing, borne and bread.
Sustain the sacrament. A child,
Before, encounters in a park
Arms that reach out to subdue.
The righteous rain falls only on
Those it chooses. O let crops grow
In this alien land of alien gods,
Unequally, as the angel passes over.

Bring wine, everything else is false.
The sky is cloudless, light translucent.
Among stones a lizard shelters.
Heat rises from the ground.
Only a beggar, emerging from a nearby cave.
It is true, the wisest among us are mad.

There is music in the distance
But nothing to see,
Enveloped in darkness.
Are they birds? Are they trees?
As I think, it fades and disappears
Leaving only the darkness,
As dense and thick as oil.
And an imagined world growing cold.

Into the tree towering in stillness,
How many thoughts of disconsolation
Sinuously entwine a bark of time,
Brittle the hopes and aspirations,
Voluminous, as they conspire
To envelop mere gestured of hands
Devoid of sympathy yet prayerful.
The gnarl, the gall, the humour
Trickling sand, and sun, dividing all
In time and space, eglantine, sharp
And penetrating. The dull words thud
Upon the forest floor, rejectamenta:
Counting, calculating; slide to oblivion.

Carrying out the corpses,
Eviscerated books,
Truncated smiles, leaves
Strewn, autumn mulch.
Regrets like snowflakes
Melting on your brow.
Necessity dissolves
Into contingency:
An image fades
Behind closed eyes.
And tomorrow, Yes
Tomorrow...how different?
You will never remember
The songthrush gone,
The world inverted,
Pleasure turned to pain,
Just...carrying out corpses.

The wind unleashed, chattering
Of teeth, wave upon wave
Of bluster, to overwhelm and
Sweep away all traces of the past,
Apart from a residual present-
Your gift to me. Hang-on there,
There will be nothing left apart
From a dream hatched from
Others' plots, carefully cultivated,
Now, battered by wind, expiring.

Hey Pagliacci, let your tears be:
Shine through, unenclouded.
With heat of the earth be comforted.
Smile, drunk, a shattered mirror.
So many fragments, so many faces.
Nothing replaces the lost object:
The grief of unrelieved longing in
The illusion of contumacy, or the
Extinction of fire, earth pacified;
Angel of longing withdrawn, in vapour.

The heron alights aloft,
Blazing radiance of time.
Less-ness, transcendence,
Beyond the rumbles of the
Forest floor, distant from
Echoes of the road that's
Travelled. Invisible to prey,
Death stalks, still, silent.
Already present, awaiting
Your disintegration. Sing,
Joyful, at the bacchanal.
The clearing under threat
Of engulfment, dark again,
Welcomes weary travails.
Cast off your clothes, dance,
As thoughts expire, mere rags,
Discarded frenzy, salubrious.

The deafmute sings,
Decomposes notes
In a league of his own.
Drowning in a surge
Of propriety acclaim,
Audience under
Capitulates in applause
Mistaken greeting. Lhasa.

Encrustations, like barnacles
On rocks, closed against life
With corpse-like vigour,
Moving mountains, dogmas:
Let everything wash over, keep
Out everything, already dead.
Nothing passing through open
Space speckled with stars.

From the distance
I can hear a sound
Approaching, a slow
Rumbling, a cosmic
Dyspepsia. Entranced
I pirouette and crouch.
Everything passes over me
And recedes; as life
Recedes. I can read
Nothing in the stars,
And only sweat on
The palms reveals
Concern. I shall be
Leaving soon, or would
Be if I were ever here,
As morning mist disperses.

Without the silence, only
Waters of forgetfulness.
Turbulence, agitation,
Fragment the crystalline
Surface; mirror onto the
Clear azure spaciousness,
At one before the eyes close.

No darkness can withstand
The presence of light.
A lighted candle can create
Shadows that move, breathe,
Embrace, until the guttering
Light splutters and stutters,
While words dissolve, and fade.

Five elements manifest in
Butter, sacramental light.
Kindness to be seen, visible
To those who see. More holy
Than outstretched hands
In supplication, receive
The gratitude of all that lives:
When we can see, nothing there.

0 goddess, radiance of my
Own inborn awareness,
Beauteous seduction
Within which I am fully
Enamoured, totally present.
As you dissolve into me
And I dissolve too, all
Is revealed as one, veil
removed, all is love, simply.

Sound, crossing between
Silence and noise,
Formed or deformed, like
Shapes shifting in a dream,
Or winter afternoon reverie,
Creating me and where I come
To belong; forever apart.
The solitary egret, white,
Along the river's bank,
Stalking what sustains it
In the shadows, beyond the light.

O sweet excess, let me drown
In your indulgence;
Blithe flames comfort me,
Effulgence of hope extinguished,
Expectations overflowing,
I am, at last, an object expressed.

Consumed with longing
Like fire;
Prisoner whose dreams
Are free,
Let my arms embrace
Expanding hope:
Infinite in finite.
The scent of honeysuckle,
Alive to demur night,
Slowly fades; the taste
Of oyster, the sea
A lost pearl. Dusk
Draws in, gathers-up
Longings, like lost days.

Diaphanous. Language drifts,
Like smoke from camp fires.
Lies fall delicate as ash.
How dense the obscurations
Have become, blackout the sun,
Leave footprints in the sky.
And, less demur than loud,
Deaf, differences go unremarked.
O this is normal: silk underwear
To wear around my face;
Innate smile through which I
Defecate what enters through
My ears. Sing: Holy, holy, holy.
Salvation is at hand. A hand that
Destroys at leisure, and for fun.

Evening scent of jasmine,
On gentle breeze excites
The senses, brings tears to eyes.
Yet recollections vanish
In eddies of a cooling stream.
Only the present is revivified.
Such poignant stillness,
Pregnant with possibility.
A tear's reflection of what
You cannot see or taste,
A smile so bitter, withered hope.

The drama unfolds
As theurgist
Evokes a presence,
Giving name and form
Which to invoke,
Benign elixirs,
And pacify our wants.
In its immediacy,
Unreadily overlooked,
I see a shape emerge
And then I vanish.
Something else is there.

Recall the past, as you might
Label a jar, *past.*
Turn it around, examine carefully,
Turn it upside down;
Everything changes, yet it is
The same, whichever way
You look- it is what you make it.

We look into each other's eyes:
What I see you couldn't comprehend,
What you smell as my identity
Would pass everyone else by.
And yet we are of one mind.
Differences conceal what is the same;
And yet not the same where there
Can be no difference, whatever is said.

I look across the slow river
To vast empty spaces
Beyond, where figures
Are lost in landscape
And landscape vanishes
Into a sky so blue,
So penetrating, like a
Gaze that becomes
What it looks at. And,
Carried on the breeze,
The sound of ancient chants,
Drums and cymbals,
Great horns and bells as if
Time meant nothing. What
Passes passes, and is present.

Come, let me dance to the toast
Of illusions, spiralling before
Control. Faust reaching for
A firmament, only within,
More sure, more meaningful
Than all that accrues. Step
Slowly, out of time, transported
Though dreams of longing for…
Raise your glasses. All is dark.

The man is without balls.
Intestate.
Showered with confetti
Of meteoric stars,
Voice with a pitch to illuminate
Submerged rocks, rainfall.

Leaving no trace, clouds
Passing, not balloons
To hold onto or some
Caricature to turn
Into an opera. Minutiae,
Microelements deposited.
Postage stamps in an album
To display and speculate.
Only making use matters,
Another verb: to charade.

*One making the mistake,*
*Is part of the mistake.*
Foxgloves now replacing
Bluebells and wild garlic.
The dance goes round
Yet you persist in going
Straight, in marching on,
Unyielding and desolate.
Tell a tale, tall of not,
Enchant and conjure up
Not forms but names
Then, reify and vivify
Those phantasms of sleep.
Bless the machine you live-in.
Having left a world behind
Construct another to inhibit.
Obscure the stars, recant
Of all you can't control.
Watching sunrise on a screen,
A shrill ululation drifts across,
Carrying benedictions of despair,
A hope for those intent to act.

There was an exclamation. It was unclear
From where, if a location
Could be
Identified. Come again.
O I don't know how do
You ever know anything?
The door slowly opened,
But the doorway was empty.
Behind him stood
A vase of flowers-
Geraniums or orchids, but not
A habitat shared.
Entwined in this knot
A kernel, or vacuous promise.

O come with me to the Blue Lagoon.
So blue, the embrace of death
Slowly enfolds you like a mother
Welcoming her wayward child.
A soothing gesture, the racing blood,
Your pure delight in finitude,
Applause of friends, despair of those
Who thought you offered more,
That you could walk on the water
Where you drown, slowly choke.
The hallowed time rising in your gorge.

As a flame gutters in the draught,
So shadows move,
Figures on the wall trapped in the dark
Thinking, *This is all.*
*This pleasure and this pain that I endure.*
As downcast eyes
Will never see the skies, or clouded skies
The sun, and I distract,
As best I can, with what comes-to-hand.
Small joys, great griefs,
Unless I chose to phantasise, and dream
Of somewhere different.
Across the seas or skies, to somewhere
Other, filled with light and colour.
To everlasting happiness that never dawns,
Missing the translucent present
While seeking recompense in sheer vacuity.
We do not see what we cannot
Look for, beyond the range we set ourselves.
Blind in our very looking, and far too distant.

Before the world began,
Before the names
That skewered shadows
And gave focus,
Allowing things, then objects
To emerge, giving
Sense and form and power
Where infants play,
Wonder existed, measureless
Movement, boundlessly
Devoid of Time and Man.

You wish to dominate,
And yet deny.
What is positive in this?
To feel secure,
Alone in grip of fear,
You calculate
And plot, yet can't control
Your tears, or tears
Of others. So superficial
The empty gesture,
As you disdainfully wave
Away, the weeping sun
When nothing more will grow.

Headland merges into sea, enthralled by mist.
The gorse and bracken damp, bejewelled.
What once was solid now dissolves in dream.
Confounded. In confusion I ask were I am.
I swirl, all other signs unsure. Boundaries
Dissolve, leaving nothing to hold onto that's
Sure. I struggle to define just what I mean,
Before words form and things receive a name.


All before me, all within; no time at all,
Nothing to discern. A magic lantern on a wall
The images of light and dust rise on a beam.
I thought I understood, but lost, mere air
In open hand; ahead a corpse-blank stare.
Let me embrace you one last time, if only
Time there was or is. I move no more than stone.
Listless the wind across the moor. Silence beyond.

# Rootless Tree

www.elysianwiles.com

www.ingramcontent.com/pod-product-compliance
Lightning Source LLC
Chambersburg PA
CBHW061032050726
47592CB00004B/1415